How to use this book::

This is a book for those who love painting. It is also suitable for writing a mood diary, and it can also be used as a card to give people. It is a unique gift.

The demo page is the original color, which is provided for your reference. It can also be used as a gift card. The painting page can be colored by referring to the demo page, but it can be changed according to your preference.

There are 5 color demonstration pages and 5 line drawing pages.

I wish you like it!

By niniN

The owner of the book:

To:

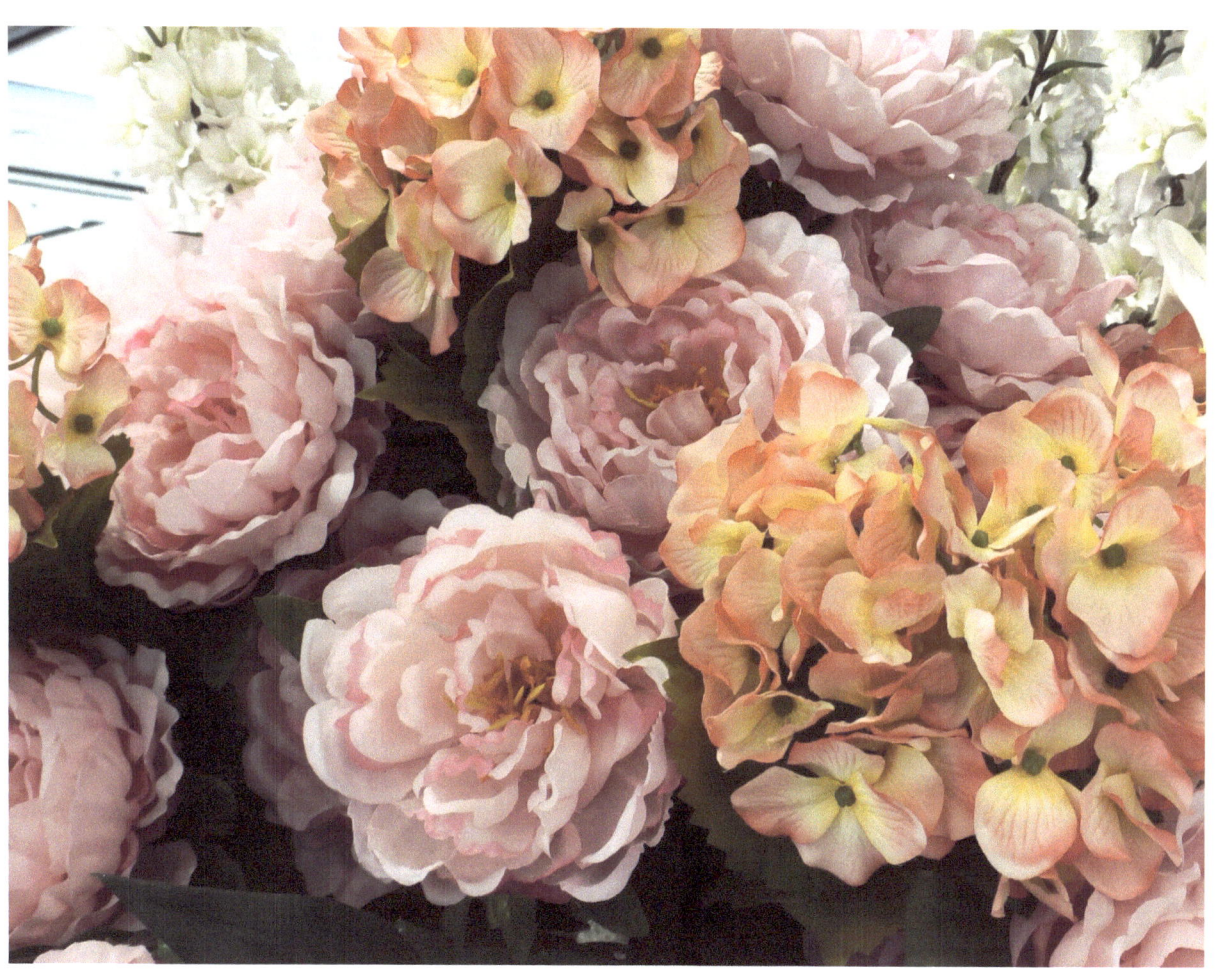

from:

To:

from:

To:

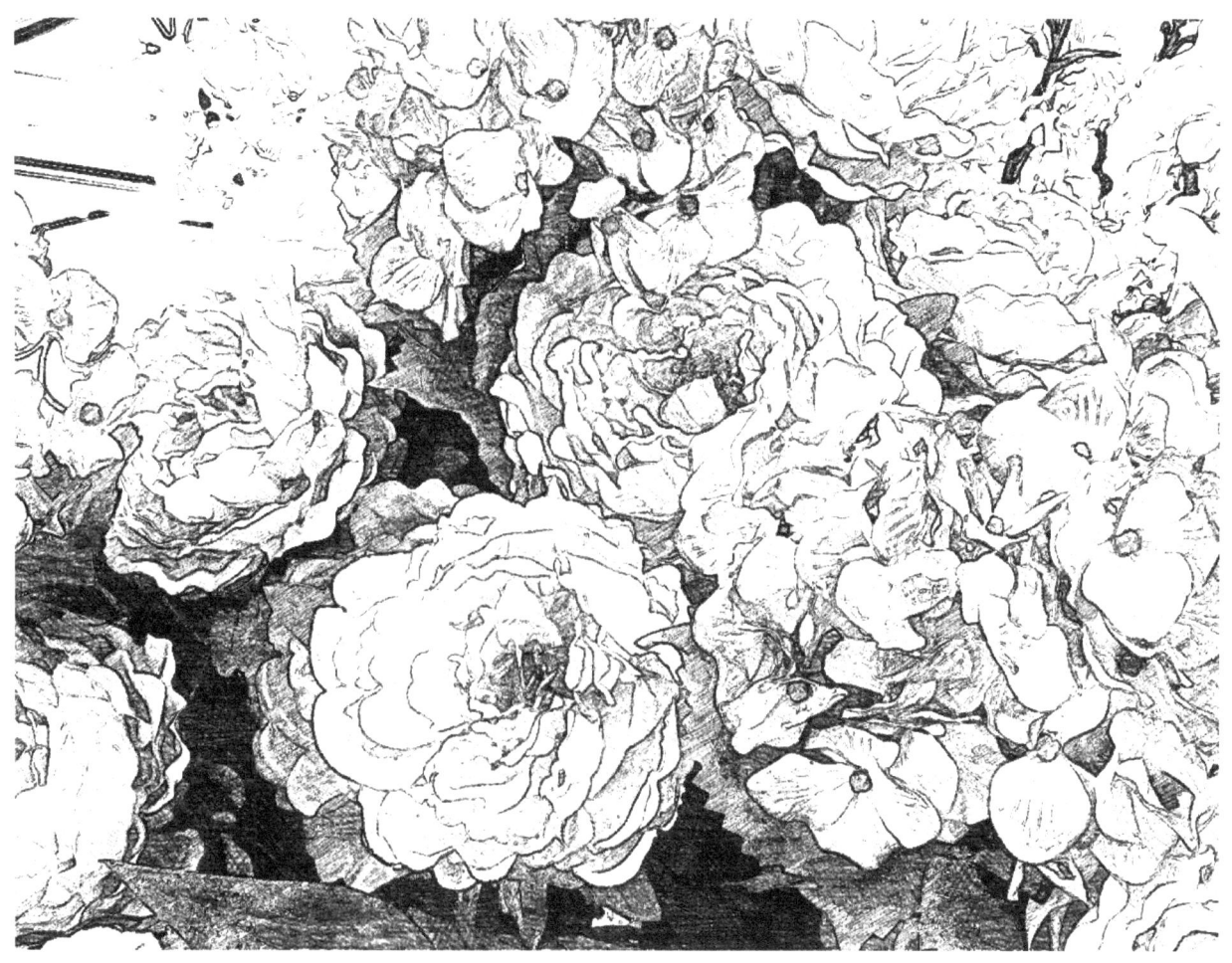

from:

To:

from:

To:

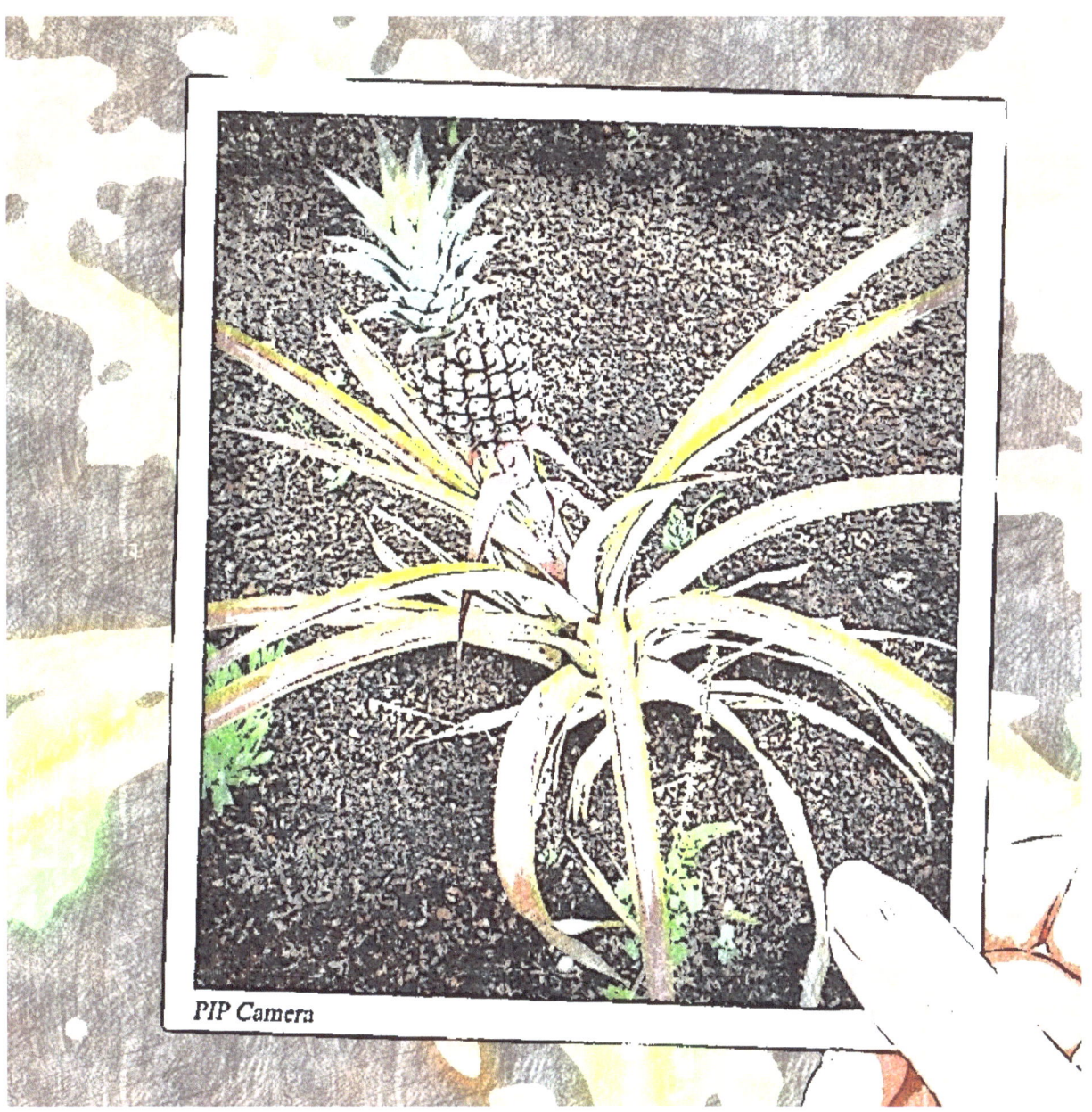

PIP Camera

from:

To:

from:

To:

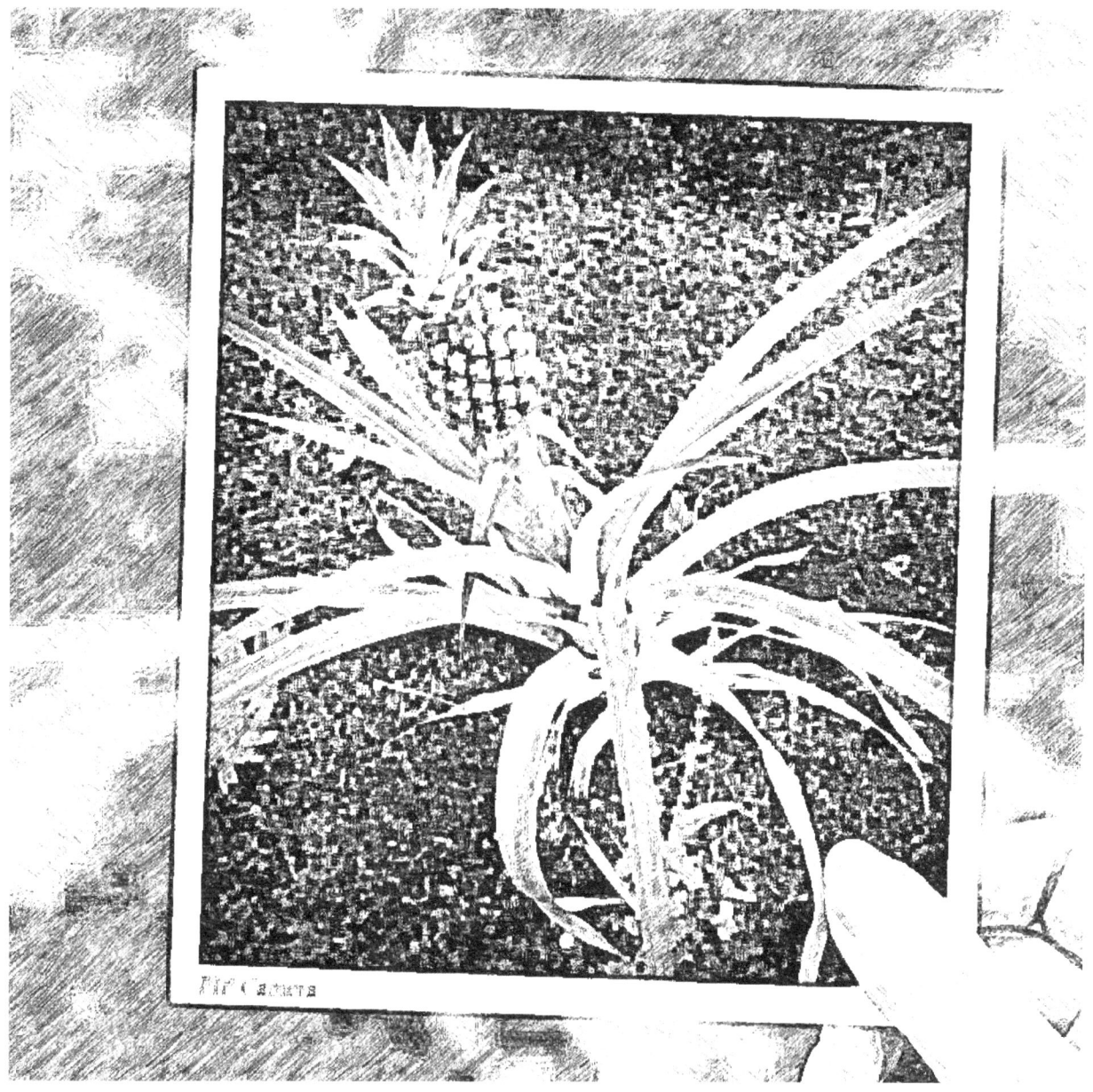

from:

To:

from:

To:

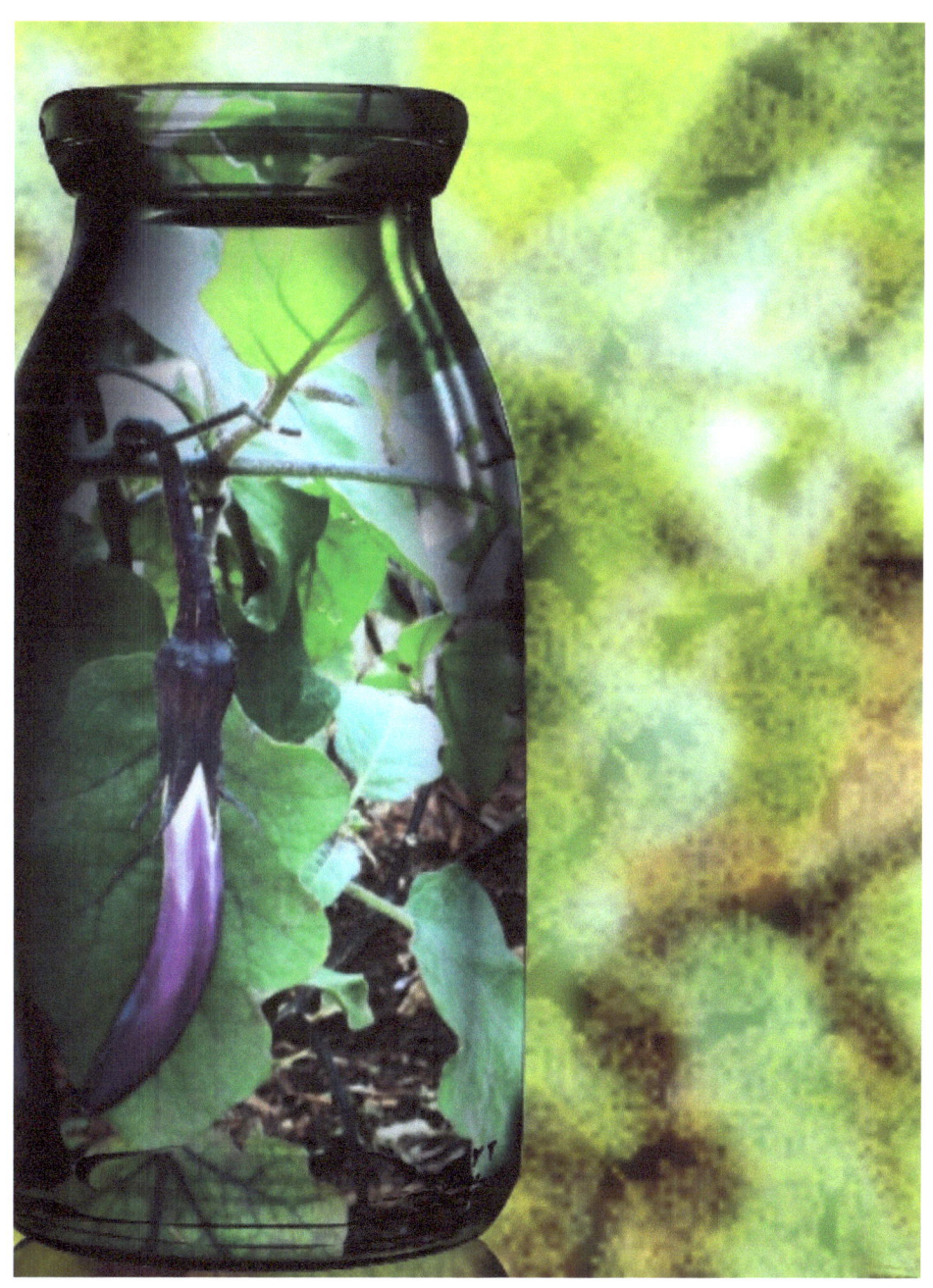

from:

To:

from:

To:

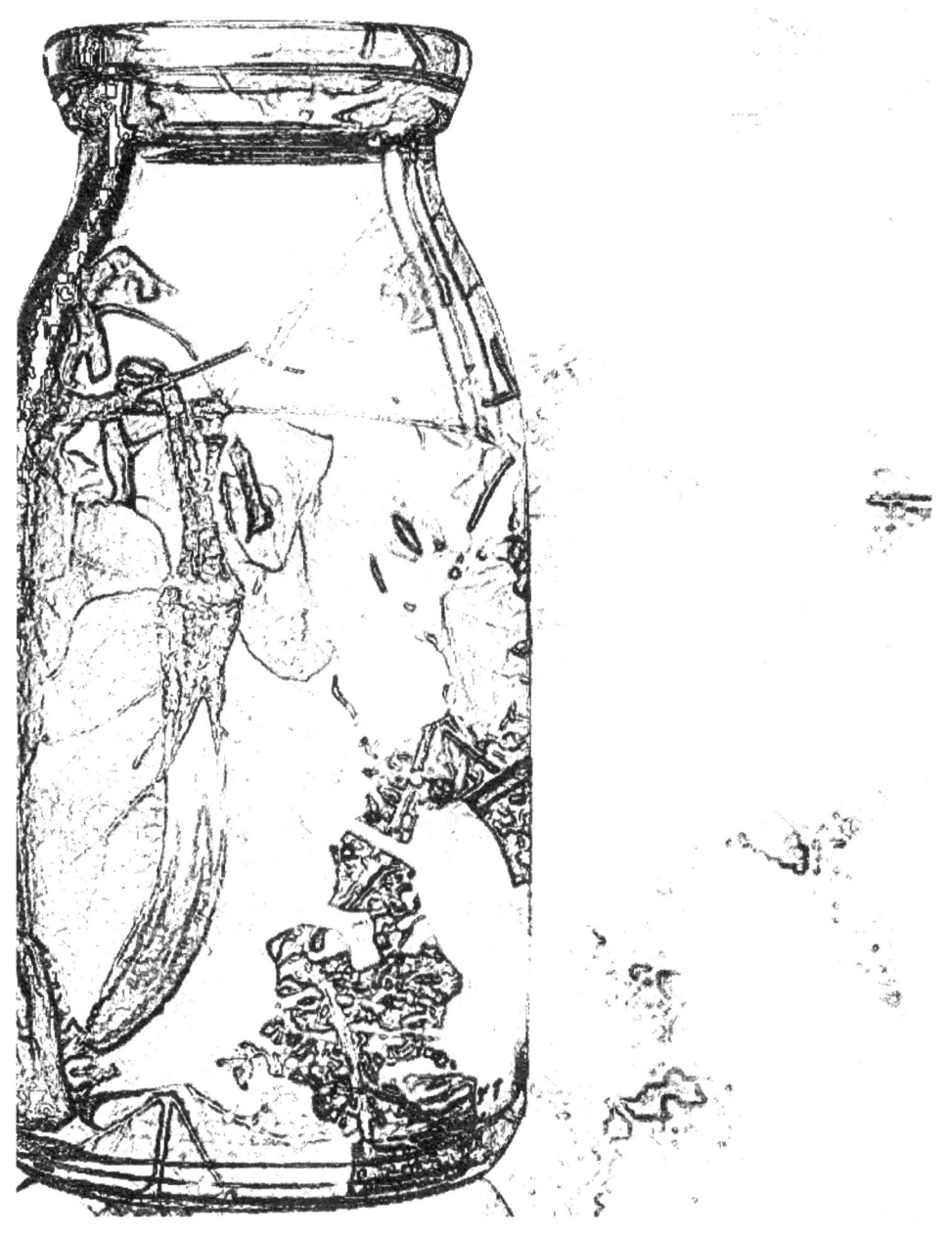

from:

To:

from:

To:

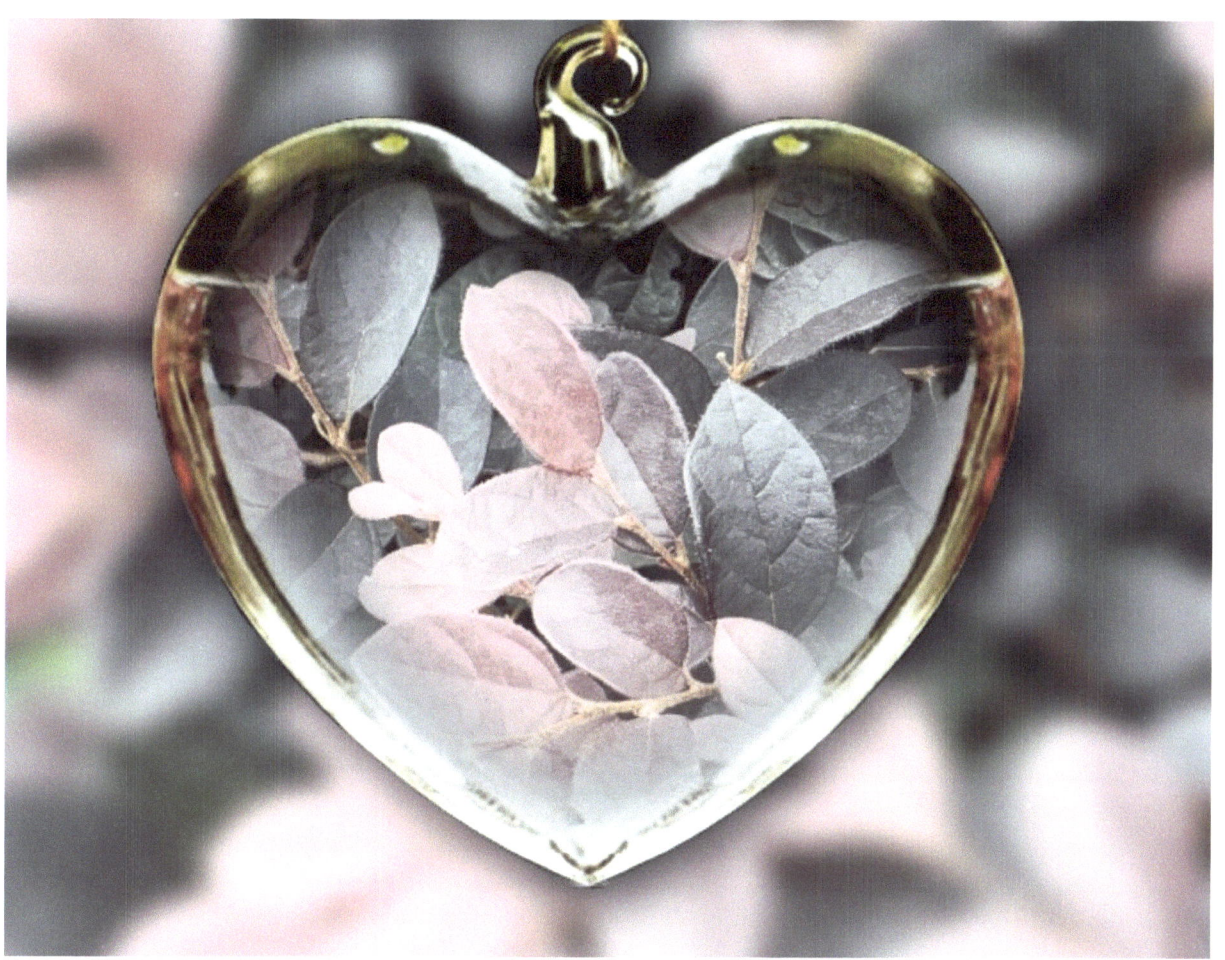

from:

To:

from:

To:

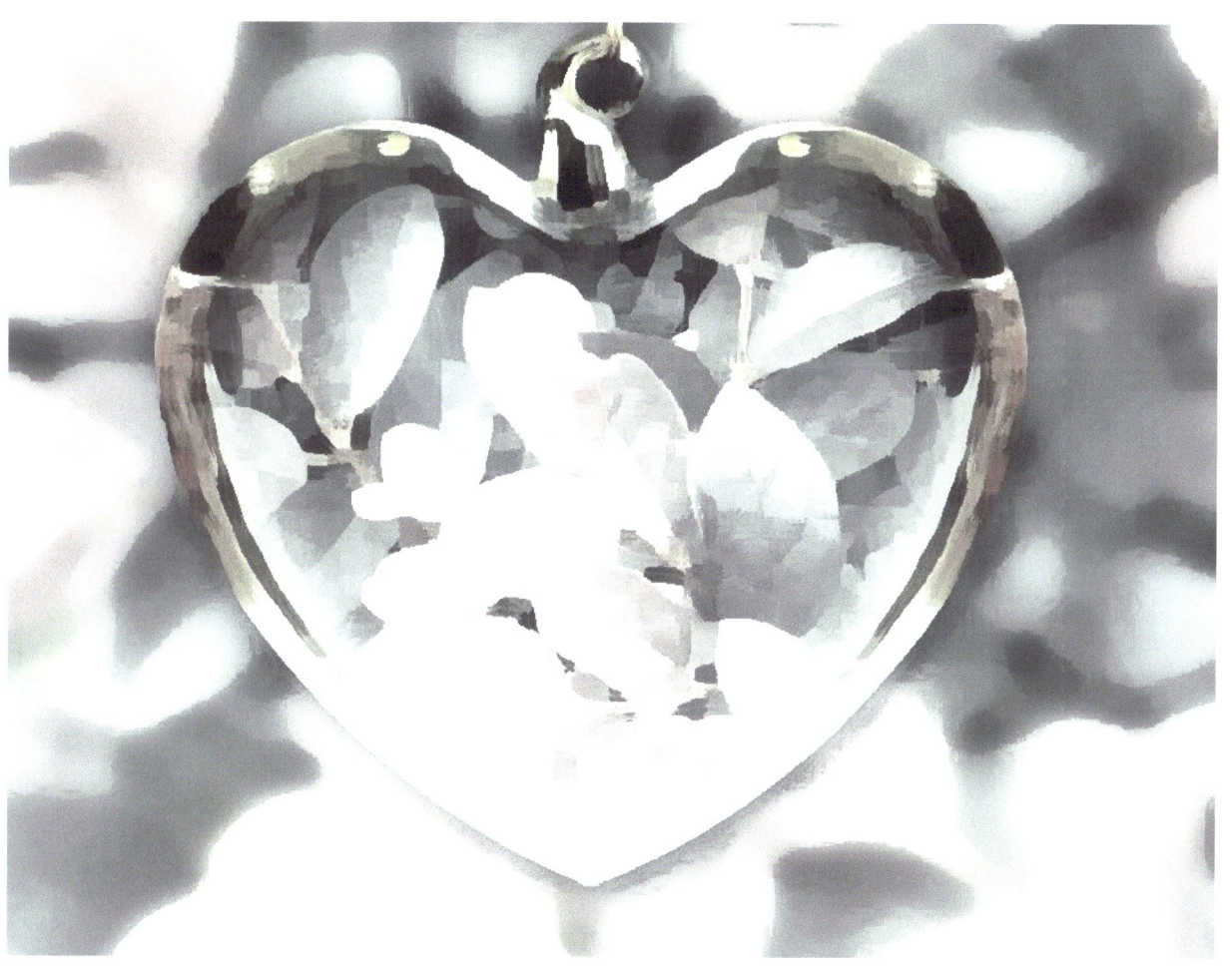

from:

To:

from:

To:

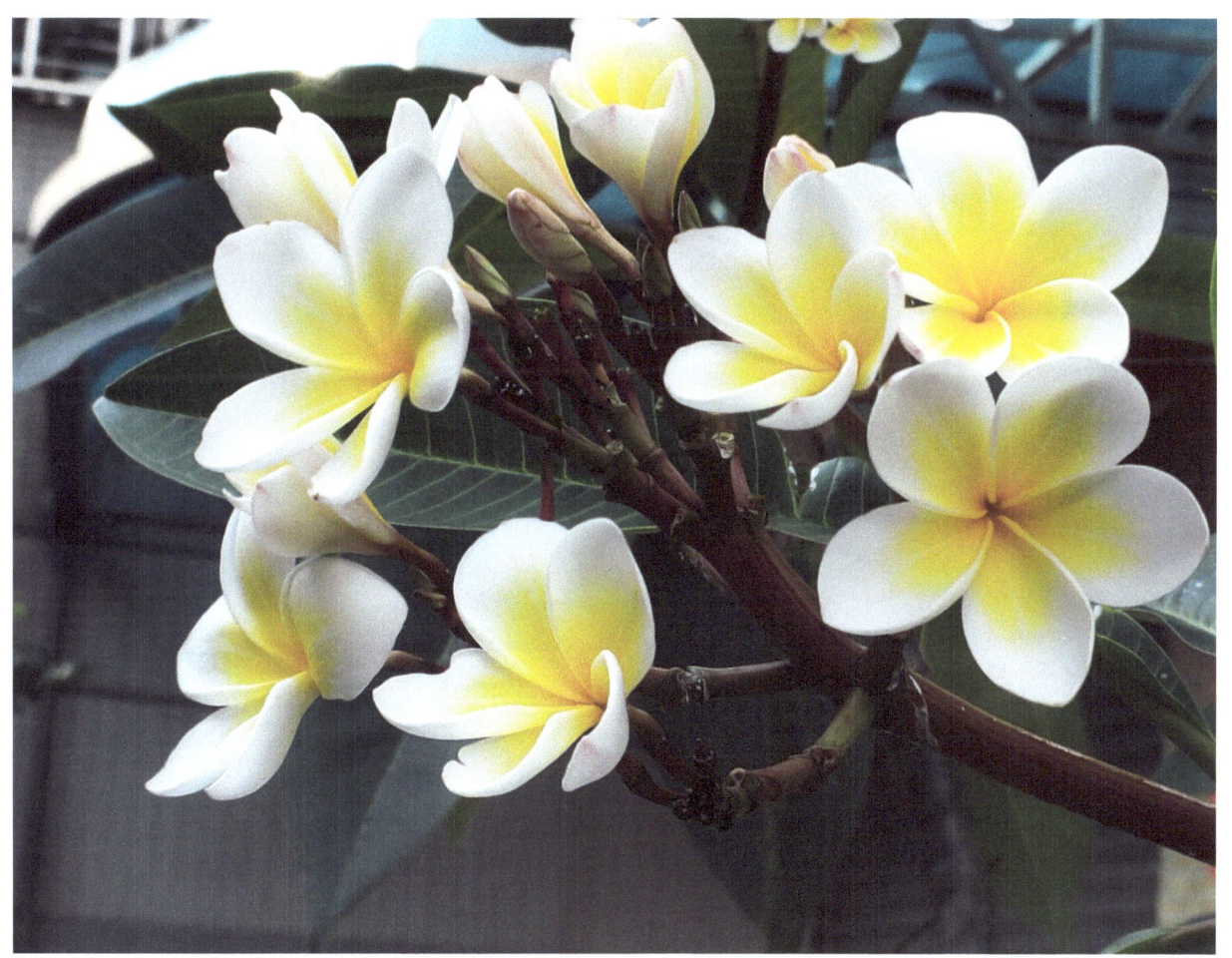

from:

To:

from:

To:

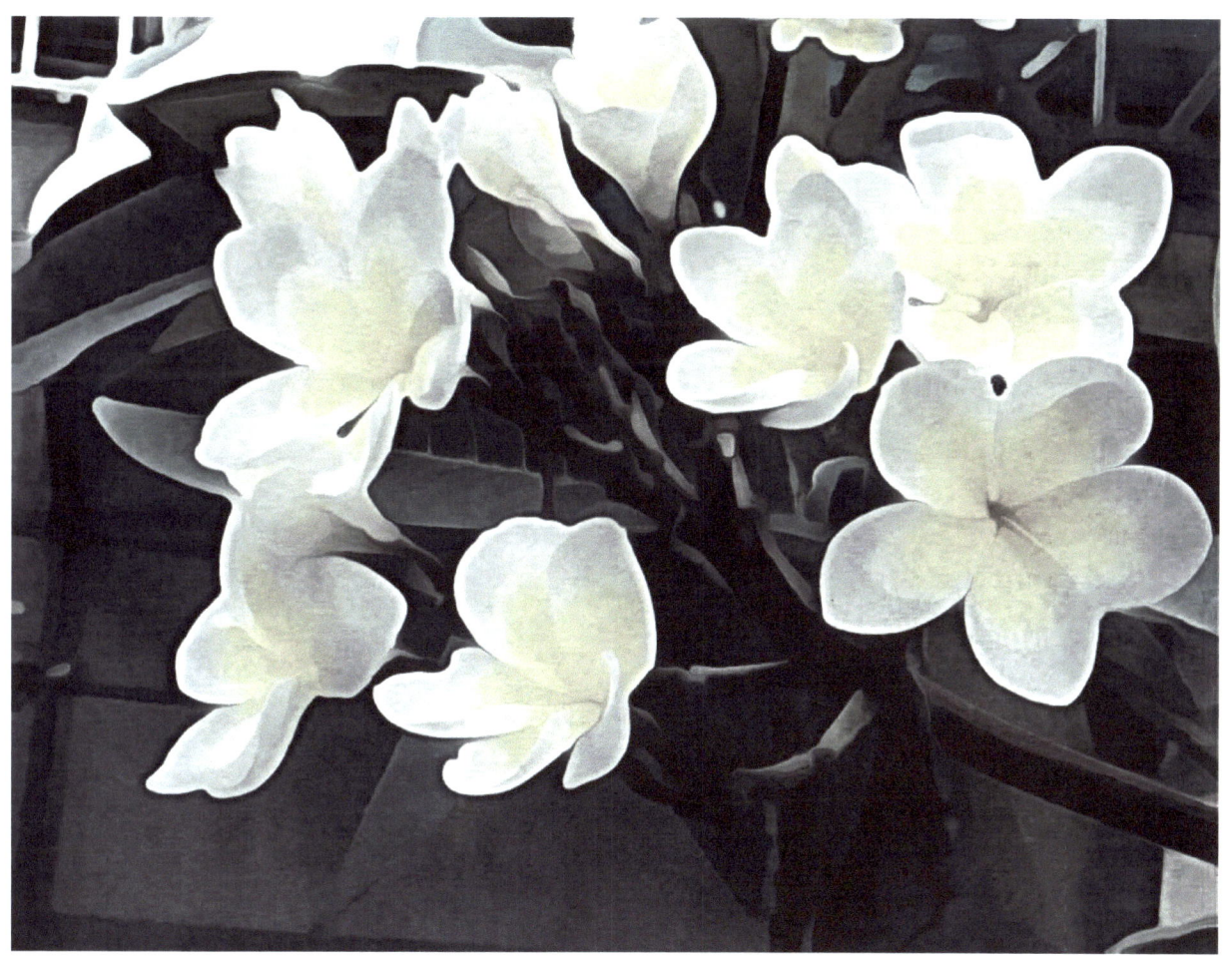

from:

To:

from:

To:

from:

To:

from: